Given

A Daily Devotional for Advent

by Mark Ryan

Published for Mark Ryan by Verité CM Ltd

Design and print management by Verité CM Ltd,
Worthing BN12 4HF
+44 (0) 1903 241975

Isaiah 9:6-7

For to us a child is born,
to us a son is given,
and the government will be on his shoulders.
And he will be called
Wonderful Counsellor, Mighty God,
Everlasting Father, Prince of Peace.
Of the greatness of his government and peace
there will be no end.
He will reign on David's throne
and over his kingdom,
establishing and upholding it
with justice and righteousness
from that time on and forever.
The zeal of the LORD Almighty
will accomplish this.

How to use this Devotional

Christmas is often a busy time for us all. This devotional is meant to be read slowly and thoughtfully to give you a spiritual oasis during the pace of the advent season. It is designed not to be too long, but it is thoughtful.

After you have read each day, sit for a few moments, and ponder what you have read. Listen if there is anything you need to pray about. The prayer at the end of each day is designed to be a prayer starter, not a whole prayer. Start with this sentence and then allow yourself to continue to pray as you feel you can.

On a day when something speaks to you especially – read that day twice. It can be a good idea to read it twice every day; once in the morning and then repeat it in the evening before bedtime.

Make your Christmas and Advent season a season of deepening your connection the One who was... Given.

First Sunday of Advent

Read the Christmas story and reflect...

Matthew 1: 18 -25

This is how the birth of Jesus the Messiah came about: His mother Mary was pledged to be married to Joseph, but before they came together, she was found to be pregnant through the Holy Spirit. Because Joseph her husband was faithful to the law, and yet did not want to expose her to public disgrace, he had in mind to divorce her quietly.

But after he had considered this, an angel of the Lord appeared to him in a dream and said, "Joseph son of David, do not be afraid to take Mary home as your wife, because what is conceived in her is from the Holy Spirit. She will give birth to a son, and you are to give him the name Jesus because he will save his people from their sins."

All this took place to fulfil what the Lord had said through the prophet: "The virgin will conceive and give birth to a son, and they will call him Immanuel" (which means "God with us").

When Joseph woke up, he did what the angel of the Lord had commanded him and took Mary home as his wife. But he did not consummate their marriage until she gave birth to a son. And he gave him the name Jesus.

Reflect:

What are the main characteristics of Joseph?

In what ways could you be faithful to what you believe, but at the same time compassionate to those who might challenge our deeply held beliefs?

As you attend a worship service today – What was the message from the service and the main lesson you could learn from it? How could you show the same compassion and wisdom of Joseph to those in your church family?

Prayer:

Father, teach me to hear what You are saying and give me the wisdom to carry it out in the way that Joseph did.

Day 2

**The Gift we did not know we needed
was given anyway...**

... a son is Given ...

When something is given, it is done so from the will of the one who wants to give it. For anything to be given, it takes the mind or heart of someone to imagine, then choose to act, and release something to another. For something to be truly given, it also has to be received. Receiving makes the act of giving complete. Being willing to receive is important, but the whole process of something being given starts outside of the ones that receive. It starts with someone noticing a need or wanting to enrich the life of another.

It is commonly said that Christmas is about giving. We exchange tokens of appreciation between us to express love to one another. This is all fine, but underneath this Advent season, with its frenetic pace of choosing that special thing for that special someone, is the deeper idea that something that all of us really need has already been given to us.

...a son is given.

Not because we asked or sought it out but because God, who loves us, decided to give us His most prized ever person. His son, the gift, is given.

This advent, let's all deepen in the idea that we are recipients of something that is given. More accurately, Someone has been given. God saw our need and decided to give the solution. What was given was given when we were not seeking it.

But given anyway.

God wanted a relationship with us because of His deep love for us. The Son was given so that we could be connected. As we enter this Advent season, let's make Advent a spiritual event. A season where we come to deepen our understanding of what is already ours... of things already given. Our spiritual shortfall is filled, the gap is closed, the strength is supplied, the love is poured. It's time we learnt to live in that which is already given instead of the striving to reach for something else.

As we start this Advent journey together, be still and take some quiet moments.

Breathe deeply, thank God that he has already supplied your greatest need. The Son is given... everything else is secondary to this.

....

Today's Truth: The Son is given, and you have become an heir in God's family.

Galatians 4:4-7:

But when the set time had fully come, God sent his Son, born of a woman, born under the law, to redeem those under the law, that we might receive adoption to sonship. Because you are his sons, God sent the Spirit of his Son into our hearts, the Spirit who calls out, "Abba, Father." So you are no longer a slave, but God's child; and since you are his child, God has made you also an heir.

Prayer: As I start this Advent season help to see the bigger picture of what you have done by sending your Son. Thank you, Father, for sending Jesus; Jesus thank you that you came.

Day 3

It's good news because there was bad news.

'For to us...'

When we introduce Christmas, we often do so by announcing that the gospel is good news. But it's only good news because there was a state of bad news that Isaiah was seeking to correct. If we ask why Isaiah began the sentence with the word 'for'... *'For to us a child is born'* ... it is another way of saying 'because to us a child is born'. Isaiah is saying, the change that is to be ushered in is going to happen because of His birth.

If we look back to Isaiah 8:22, it speaks of distress and darkness and fearful gloom, then Isaiah, from chapter 9, introduces that this darkness will be dispelled, and oppression will be broken (Isaiah 9:4), opposition will be crushed, (Isaiah 9:5). How? Because (for) *to us a child is born, to us a son is given!* The Son will bring the change of government and spiritual power to break the oppression and shine a light in the gloom.

Without falling into excessive negativity or a 'poor me' mentality, we need to appreciate the trouble we are in before we met Jesus. We need to see the absolute necessity of the Advent of Christ. Before we can move on to things like the Christmas film, or the number one, or peace on earth and goodwill, or charity projects, or the magic of Christmas, or stardust and twinkles, or whatever other Christmas attachment you have to this season, let us firstly understand that Jesus was on a rescue mission to shatter and solve a completely desperate state of affairs.

We were walking in complete darkness, and all our decisions and outlook were twisted by the sin we participated in. This is why Isaiah opens chapter 9:2 with *'The people walking in darkness have seen a great light; on those living in the land of deep darkness a light has dawned'.* We needed light. The New Testament confirms that nothing has changed in our natural state, it says in Ephesians 5:8 *"For you were once darkness, but now you are light in the Lord. Live as children of light"* ...Because the Son is given, we can now have light, but our natural state is darkness, oppression, and gloom.

As we continue in the Advent season don't allow yourself to become complacent about the natural state of the world without Christ. We have the light, but those around us are in darkness. Let's remember the bad news so we don't forget to share the Good News! Let's be thankful we have seen the light!

....

Today's Truth: Darkness only disappears if we allow the light to shine to dispel it.

Matthew 5:14-16:

You are the light of the world. A town built on a hill cannot be hidden. Neither do people light a lamp and put it under a bowl. Instead, they put it on its stand, and it gives light to everyone in the house. In the same way, let your light shine before others, that they may see your good deeds and glorify your Father in heaven.

Prayer: Father, help me share Your light with a friend.

Day 4

It's personal...

'For to Us.'

If we are not careful, we can turn Christmas into general ideas of good feelings and being friendly to everyone. We hear it often said, 'well if you can't help someone out at Christmas, then, when can you?'. Or we hear politicians giving a Christmas message about how we can help each other or do better. There are many general concepts of peace and making a better world at Christmas. Charity and helping is on the agenda.

There is no doubt that helping out is a good thing, but before we rush to seeing the need in others, let's remember the Jesus was sent to US. *For to us a child is born, to us, a son is given...*

On this day in Advent, think about your own relationship with Jesus. He came for you. When Jesus was born, you were his mission. He did many things and taught lots of things, but everything was done so that you could connect with God. You are the US in this announcement.

Advent is a season to remember that you are especially chosen by God. We are to live in this chosenness. This is, firstly, a mindset, that your primary belonging is to God. He came for you. Before anyone has a call on your life, He does. Also, chosenness is expressed by our priorities: if He came for me, then I will arrange my life around where He is taking me.

We are not only chosen by Him, but He is also given to us.

He is the Gift to us to fill our lives with His presence and love. We are chosen, He is given. We are called upon to live our lives for Him, but all of our efforts are fuelled by the incredible grace poured out upon us.

Christmas is a time to strengthen your personal relationship with the One who was given specifically for us. If you want to strengthen this personal connection, be personal with Him by telling Him your deepest needs, thoughts, and desires. Lots of people will make wishes for Christmas, but you can make a personal request to the One who can actually do something about it. Don't hold back; tell Him what is really on your heart.

Make it personal.

....

Today's truth: Remember you are His target. You are His goal, so, get real, up close and personal with Him.

Ezekiel 34:11-12:

For this is what the Sovereign Lord says: I myself will search for my sheep and look after them. As a shepherd looks after his scattered flock when he is with them, so will I look after my sheep. I will rescue them from all the places where they were scattered on a day of clouds and darkness.

Prayer: Draw me close to you as I draw near to you.

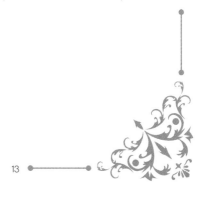

Day 5

Born like no other birth in the history of births!

'A child is born...'

Jesus was not sent to appear as an angel might have been; instead He was born. He travelled through a birth canal from his temporary home of a womb. He was flesh and blood like you and me. He had to be born; otherwise, the plan would be incomplete and flawed. The idea that Jesus was incarnated, or became flesh is a necessary mystery. He had to be human so that he can experience everything we go through, yet without being tainted and flawed by the sin that inhabits us. He had to be human so that we can be confident in approaching Him knowing that He *'sympathises with our weaknesses'* (see Hebrews 4:15).

But the real wonder of this Christmas season is to ponder the mystery of what it could be like for the eternal God to limit Himself to the human condition and experience. It's hard to explain, but Jesus was really a baby, letting go of His power and wisdom, setting this aside so He could learn and grow as we do. He was fully divine at the same time as fully human, but as a full human He did experience our weakness and limitation. His divine nature allowed this and did not compromise it... it truly is a great mystery.

But here is the real Advent lesson for us. Jesus accepted this limitation. Is it time that we embraced our limitations? Much of our teaching is about breaking our limitations into a higher life, but what the incarnation teaches us is that it is appropriate to embrace limitation so that we can walk deeper into God's will. As you accept your healthy limitations, you will learn how to live your life by faith. You will learn how to trust God for strength and protection, and so your life will not always be pressured by the strength of your performance.

For to us a child is born... for us, the eternal the God accepts limitation so that He can model a life of faith. Is there something in your life that you are fighting against, and yet you need to allow it to teach you its lessons? Is there a limitation around you that, if you are honest, is actually doing you good? Is there a healthy limitation that you are so set on changing that you are missing the richness of its wisdom?

It's hard to be limited, but you can take these frustrations and feelings to Jesus because more than anyone, He knows how you feel because He has experienced the greatest limitation in the history of the world.

....

Today's Truth: Your limits can be God's levers to achieve greater things through you.

Hebrews 2:14-15:

Since the children have flesh and blood, he too shared in their humanity so that by his death he might break the power of him who holds the power of death—that is, the devil— and free those who all their lives were held in slavery by their fear of death.

Prayer: Father, as I look over my life, give me the wisdom to accept that which I should not change until the right time.

Day 6

Sonship.

'To us a son is given...'

In describing the gift of Jesus as a 'son', the Bible is saying something special. As a human son of the carpenter, Jesus was entering into the human experience where He would have to grow in wisdom and stature and find His place in the world around Him. To be a son means that Jesus was put on a learning journey. The Bible even deepens this idea of sonship in Jesus by saying, *'Son though he was, he learned obedience from what he suffered,'* (Hebrews 5 :8). To be a son meant that Jesus was just like us in that He had to grow and learn things.

But being a son also meant that Jesus had the spiritual status of sonship. He would inherit the kingdom that God had planned. Our theme scripture from Isaiah makes it abundantly clear that this was no ordinary son, but someone who would not only be instrumental in bringing about the Kingdom of God but that He would rule and reign in it. He was the heir to the throne that would never pass away. As a son, He has the authority of a King. Being a son meant the status of sonship.

The word 'son' in the original Hebrew also has the shade of meaning that he is a builder, or more accurately, it would be through Him that the future kingdom would be built. For the Hebrews, a son was the builder of generations. When Jesus is described as son, He, therefore has a mission to build that family that would live out and be the Kingdom of God on earth. This was His mission.

When God confers on us that we are also the sons of God, (not gender specific), we are also receiving these three aspects of the sonship that was conferred on Jesus. We are to grow and learn what it means to follow God, and so, we will be subject to different seasons that will bring the best out of us. We have the status of being a son of God, and therefore, we are heirs of God's promises. As sons too, we have a mission to build the future generations that will inhabit the kingdom of God.

In this special season, take a moment to embrace your sonship in God. What is your current or next learning experience in God? If you had to name it today, what is it that you are learning or you need to learn? What promises, as God's beloved child, do you need to claim? Is there part of your spiritual inheritance that you are not claiming? Sonship is your status, walk in it! In Advent, can you express your sonship by seeking to build the kingdom of the Father? Could you invite someone to hear the Christmas story?

....

Today's Truth: A learning journey, sonship status, and the mission to build are all part of you being the beloved and chosen son of God.

Romans 8:14-16:

For those who are led by the Spirit of God are the children of God. The Spirit you received does not make you slaves, so that you live in fear again; rather, the Spirit you received brought about your adoption to sonship. And by him we cry, "Abba, Father." The Spirit himself testifies with our spirit that we are God's children.

Prayer: Father, let me live as a son, not a slave.

Day 7

Shoulders that carry the weight of the world.

'Government will be on his shoulders...'

You may have heard the traditional song 'He's got the whole world in his hands, He's got you and me sister in His hands,' etc. More precisely however, Jesus has the whole world on His shoulders! He 'shoulders' the responsibility for how the Kingdom is led. The government of God is not like our government that administers policies. The government, as Jesus does it, is more about ruling and directing. Government in this way is having dominion over all that is under it. The force of what is meant by this government is strong. It means that Jesus will take responsibility and lead definitely; it isn't a democracy but a rule where He is in charge. We see this at the end of time as Jesus judges the earth. But here, we also see that this government is to be recognised in the waiting time, before the conclusion of the age.

There is a beautiful intertwining of thought about the government resting on the shoulders of Jesus. In order to usher in this government, Jesus allowed the cross to rest on His shoulders. This was the pathway to create the Kingdom, so that He could govern the hearts of men and women. The shoulders that were prepared to bear the cross are now worthy to have the government of the Kingdom resting upon Him.

There is a further and more interesting word play in the Hebrew concerning the word 'government'. The root of the word 'government' means 'to contend', but with Jesus, there is no contention about it; the government merely rests upon Him because that is where all government rightly belongs. Government fits on Him like a robe.

As we move deeper into this Advent season, it can be a time of high activity as we seek to wrap things up well before Christmas. We may be engaged in last minute shopping or arranging travel plans. It's far from peaceful. Our nation and the world have been beset with extreme events and strife over this year.

We need to hear the voice of our loving God say to us 'I've got this'. Stop striving. It's time to turn our hearts towards His government, and allow Him to direct us. As the government rests on His shoulders, it is time for us to rest in His government. As we do this, we are carried on His shoulders. One by one take all your concerns off your shoulders and place them upon His.

....

Today's Truth: God's government is the pathway to your health.

1 Peter 5:7:

Cast all your anxiety on him because he cares for you.

Prayer: Drop thy still dews of quietness till all our strivings cease, take from our souls the strain and stress and let our ordered lives confess, the beauty of thy peace. – from the hymn 'Dear Lord and Father of mankind.'

Second Sunday of Advent

Read the Christmas story and reflect...

Luke 2:1-21

In those days a decree went out from Caesar Augustus that the whole empire should be registered. This first registration took place while Quirinius was governing Syria. So everyone went to be registered, each to his own town.

Joseph also went up from the town of Nazareth in Galilee, to Judea, to the city of David, which is called Bethlehem, because he was of the house and family line of David, to be registered along with Mary, who was engaged to him[c] and was pregnant. While they were there, the time came for her to give birth. Then she gave birth to her firstborn son, and she wrapped him tightly in cloth and laid him in a manger, because there was no guest room available for them. In the same region, shepherds were staying out in the fields and keeping watch at night over their flock. Then an angel of the Lord stood before them, and the glory of the Lord shone around them, and they were terrified. But the angel said to them, "Don't be afraid, for look, I proclaim to you good news of great joy that will be for all the people: Today in the city of David a Savior was born for you, who is the Messiah, the Lord. This will be the sign for you: You will find a baby wrapped tightly in cloth and lying in a manger."

Suddenly there was a multitude of the heavenly host with the angel, praising God and saying: Glory to God in the highest heaven, and peace on earth to people he favors!

When the angels had left them and returned to heaven, the shepherds said to one another, "Let's go straight to Bethlehem and see what has happened, which the Lord has made known to us."

They hurried off and found both Mary and Joseph, and the baby who was lying in the manger. After seeing them, they reported the message they were told about this child, and all who heard it were amazed at what the shepherds said to them. But Mary was treasuring up all these things in her heart and meditating on them. The shepherds returned, glorifying and praising God for all the things they had seen and heard, which were just as they had been told. When the eight days were completed for his circumcision, he was named Jesus – the name given by the angel before he was conceived.

....

Reflect: In this passage we see the Shepherds who are willing to enquire and to see what Jesus was like, and we see Angels in full worship.

As we journey through this Advent season can you also combine both seeking Him and worship to Him? This combination of humble, obedient seeking and extravagant worship will lead you to a deeper discovery of Jesus. He is the reason for this season... find Him.

As you attend a worship service today – What was the message from the service and the main lesson you could learn from it?

Prayer: Please let me seek like a Shepherd, and worship like an Angel.

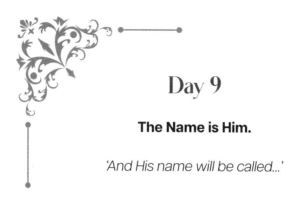

Day 9

The Name is Him.

'And His name will be called...'

Many of us have chosen names for our children, or we have been named after someone. When choosing names, we often select a name that we either like, or a name that signifies something that we hope the child will become. Our naming is aspirational or based on preference. Names in the Bible, however, are different; they are more descriptive of what the person is like. They serve as labels for their character. One prime example in the Old Testament is Abigail's first husband, Nabal, whose name means 'foolish'. He certainly lived out this character in his dealing with David (See 1 Samuel 25).

The Names of God are the purest example of this. They describe who He is, not what we hope Him to be. Any name used for God tells us His essential nature, character, and identity. While we might have a name that we do not live up to, in God's case, He actually displays the name that He bears; it is who He truly is and how He behaves. So when Isaiah tells us that we shall 'call His name,' and then goes on to list several names, he is not just describing how we will identify Him, but how we are to know Him and relate to Him. Isaiah is showing us what Christ is like, what His very essence is. He isn't just called Wonderful; He is actually wonderful by nature. He isn't just called a Counsellor, wisdom and counsel flow from His very nature. When He is called Mighty God, it's not just praise from an adoring prophet; He actually possesses mighty power in His being and nature. In naming Him eternal

Father, it means that His existence is eternal. Calling Him the Prince of Peace describes that by nature, God can dispense peace to any soul and cause peace to happen; He has the authority to dispel turbulence.

His name is His nature. This means we can know what He is like and, consequently, how to relate to Him and what to expect from Him. God cannot be what He is not, but His names tell us what and who He is. When we understand the full meaning of His Name, we can then begin to say to ourselves, 'If He is really like that, then surely I can trust who He is.'

What is your perception and image of God? Does it come from the wrong source, or from some abusive authority in your history? The names of God act as a lens through which we can see Him. Is it time to look at God not through your history or perhaps some difficult relationships, but to see Him again as He really is? Here is a key to health in your life. When you see God properly, you can begin to see yourself as God sees you, and to begin to behave the way He wants you to, from a place of healing. Let's align ourselves with how God truly is, and then we can be who we really are. By seeing God properly, we will then learn to relate to Him in healthy ways, and as a result, rid ourselves of habits and attitudes that are detrimental to us.

....

Today's Truth: His Name is His Character that you can trust.

Psalm 9:10: *Those who know your name trust in you, for you, Lord, have never forsaken those who seek you.*

Matthew 1:21b: *...you are to give him the name Jesus, because he will save his people from their sins.*

Prayer: Father, teach me the truth of Your names, so I may know You better.

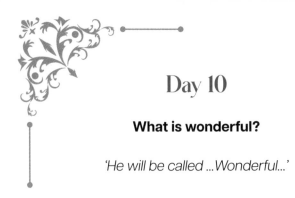

Day 10

What is wonderful?

'He will be called ...Wonderful...'

The latest IKEA slogan for their furniture concepts is 'The Wonderful Everyday'. It's a pleasant idea, but for something to be wonderful, it cannot be routine and everyday. The Hebrew root to this description of the coming Jesus is that He is extraordinary, miraculous, and unusual. That Jesus is Wonderful makes Him hard to understand; we cannot confine Him within a box that we can keep safe. He cannot be contained in these ways.

As Wonderful, He does wonders. He accomplishes things that cannot be done in the natural way of working things out; they are miracles. To be Wonderful means He is astonishing and sets Himself apart from others through the remarkable acts He performs. When we speak of God in such glowing terms, we are often tempted to balance it with statements about our need for faithfulness when it seems that God is not working His wonders. Because we live in a very challenging world, we are right to call for faithfulness even when we don't see God performing His marvellous, miraculous, and wonderful acts. But just for a moment, step back and consider that He calls Himself Wonderful. This means that nothing that you are facing is beyond His grasp or power to change.

As Christians, we are encouraged to have healthy habits and routines. We all benefit from consistency, but when we only adhere to correct routines, we risk taking the wonder out of our experience and seeing things solely as the product of good disciplines. We need to be open to the miraculous We cannot live in denial, and our situations may indeed be tough, but we also shouldn't live in a monochrome world where we never anticipate the intervention of a Wonderful God who performs wonders! Is it time to step back and look for the Wonderful God in your situation? It was the English poet Willian Cowper who coined the phrase 'God moves in mysterious ways His wonders to perform.' The wonderful can happen in your ordinary life if you are open to inviting God to do what only He can do.

The Christmas story is all about how God invades the harsh realities of our world. God in flesh now appearing, looking like an ordinary baby, will have a ministry filled with wonders. This season of Advent is a time for us to invite the Wonderful into the depths of our dark winters, allowing our perception to change and be open to even the smallest of miracles in our everyday situations.

You may not experience the Wonderful every day, but every day you can know Him who is Wonderful. And when you do this, the wonderful shows up on the days you least expect it.

....

Todays Truth: God changes our perspective on problems when we alter our perception of how He can be involved.

Isaiah 55: 8-9:

'For my thoughts are not your thoughts, neither are your ways my ways,' declares the Lord. 'As the heavens are higher than the earth, so are my ways higher than your ways and my thoughts than your thoughts.'

Prayer: Despite the evidence to the contrary, I choose to believe and invite You to be Wonderful and perform wonders in my situations.

Day 11

Counsellor: wisdom for life.

'And he will be called... Counsellor'.

It could be said that when we are young, we frequently seek power, but as we get older, we start asking for wisdom. We come to realise that our greater need is the insight required to carry out our responsibilities, and the power to do it becomes a secondary concern.

We tend to want God to provide us ready-made answers and formulas, but what He promises as the title 'Counsellor' is actually someone who consults with you, and comes alongside you to speak life wisdom for specific situations. The Bible itself is wisdom upon which to build our lives, but God also intends to make both the wisdom of the Bible, and the Spirit-inspired wisdom, applicable to your specific life context when you need it.

This is a rich promise that underscores how much of a relationship God desires to have with you. 'Counsellor' means Jesus is inviting you to talk, commune, and work things out with Him in process. The counsel and wisdom that God provides is not just about offering answers, but also about helping you understand yourself and why you might want to go in a certain direction.

So today, if you are seeking wisdom and direction, the first step is to be honest with yourself and ask what your preferred outcome or direction is, and then to present this to the Lord. Without honesty, He cannot direct you. As the Counsellor, He wants to advise and consult so that you grow as a person. Merely revealing an answer without teaching you something about yourself very rarely happens with Jesus.

The good news is that the counsel of Jesus is not limited to the historical record of His words, as precious as they are. He also promised *'Another Counsellor'* who would dwell within us (John 14:16). So, this sense of walking with us to advise, consult, and counsel is ever-present and always available.

An important aspect of the wisdom promised to us is that it is counter-cultural to what the world might offer. God's wisdom may appear as foolishness to the world. The wisdom provided helps us understand what we have received in Jesus and how to live it out in the context of the world's situation. When refering to Jesus as Counsellor, it's not merely self-help or life tips; it's revelation and insight into how God wants you to live. As such, it may come at a cost and be contrary to what those in the world might advise you. It becomes crucial to evaluate the guidance we receive from non-Spirit filled people.

....

Today's truth: The Counsellor gives wisdom that is appropriate to your context. He consults rather than just directs and His wisdom is always counter cultural.

1 Corinthians 2:10-12:

The Spirit searches all things, even the deep things of God. For who knows a person's thoughts except their own spirit within them? In the same way no one knows the thoughts of God except the Spirit of God. What we have received is not the spirit of the world, but the Spirit who is from God, so that we may understand what God has freely given us.

Prayer: I invite You, O Counsellor, to walk with me and provide insight that I cannot see without You.

Day 12

The Warrior... your Champion.

'And he will be called Mighty God'.

In the Christmas season, rightly, we often focus upon the humanity of Jesus. He is seen as the vulnerable baby in the stable, identifying with us. However, Isaiah directs our attention away from this momentarily because he wants us to see the true nature of Jesus. We must recognise the deity of Jesus. Jesus is not merely a prophet or a good man; He is very God. While there may be other places to delve into proof concerning the deity of Christ, here in Isaiah, He is simply declared to us as the Mighty God. There are no excuses or arguments, He is God, and the God is Mighty to act and save! No further explanation is needed.

This is the description of Jesus as Warrior like, and it moves us away from the meek and mild perception. We are directed toward the mighty worker of miracles. In the book of Acts 10:38, Jesus is described as, *'God anointed Jesus of Nazareth with the Holy Spirit and power, and how he went around doing good and healing all who were under the power of the devil, because God was with Him.'* The original Hebrew word for mighty conveys more than mere heroism; it represents valiance, might, and strength in military leadership. He is a brave and powerful leader that leads the armies of God like no other King before Him. Truly, C.S. Lewis' portrayal of Jesus as the mighty Lion is accurate in that 'He is a good Lion, but He is not safe.'

We know that during His earthly ministry, Jesus exhibited humble and servant leadership, but we must not mistake this for weakness or an inability to face challenges. He confronted opposition and took on spiritual powers, stripping them of their power. As we are deep into this Advent season, where many of us long for rest after the preparations leading up to Christmas, one lesson we must reflect on is whether we've been trying to confine this mighty God within a box. Keeping God within the convenient spaces of our lives never works; eventually, He will break out.

As we rest and reflect at the end of the year, it might be time to make a fresh commitment to go with the flow of when God is moving and not hold back. It can be unnerving and requires faith to follow where God is leading, but going with it is our best option. Decide to flow with the power and guidance of the Warrior who is fighting not only your battles but is also working to establish more of His kingdom in the people around you. Whatever He tells you to do, after reflection and counsel, do it! He cannot be the Mighty God to you if your constant response is "I might not, God!"

....

Today's Truth: Let's not seek to confine God within the limits of our lifestyle but rather be consumed by living according to His will.

Zephaniah 3:17:

The Lord your God is with you, the Mighty Warrior who saves. He will take great delight in you; in his love he will no longer rebuke you, but will rejoice over you with singing.

Prayer: Father, please reveal to me where I might be confining You instead of following You.

Day 13

Eternal nurturing.

'And he shall be called... Everlasting Father.'

This is a beautiful depiction of Jesus with a twofold meaning. It literally means 'the Father of eternity,' which firstly signifies that He inhabits or possesses eternity. It speaks to His pre-existent nature of always being with God an where God is.

Daniel saw Jesus as the *Ancient of Days* (Daniel 7); Isaiah looked up and saw *Him seated on the throne, filling the entire temple* (Isaiah 6); John referred to Him as the *Word that was with God, and without Him, nothing was made that is made* (John 1). When the Bible calls Him the 'firstborn over all creation', this is not a title denoting being born first, but rather a title of honour and prominence, having all the authority. As the writer to the Hebrew puts it, 'But about the Son He says, *"Your throne, O God, will last for ever and ever"'*; (Hebrews 1:8). This description signifies that Jesus has eternity in his hands and has been forever.

When we combine this eternal description with His designation as Father, we see the true heart of Jesus towards us. Some have struggled with the description of Jesus as Father because they fear it might dilute the teaching on the Trinity. However, this is not a description of status or position; it is a description of nature and function. Calling Jesus Father means He is loving and tender, compassionate and an all-wise Instructor. Just like a father, He trains us in the ways of God and provides for our needs. He is eternally nurturing towards us. It is indeed a beautiful description. There is never a moment in all of time when He does not want to Father us.

Today, you might find yourself caught up in the temporary. The challenges of today may be drowning out the larger picture of God's love and care for you. Take some moments to reflect on the eternal nature of Jesus. Nothing will surprise Him; He has seen it all coming. He has your nurture in His heart. From His pre-existent state, He has always intended to provide, guide, feed, and fill you. By nature, He knows how to nurture. His character is such that He knows what you need. He is capable and intelligent enough to work out what you need, but more than this, in His heart, He wants to meet your need because He simply wants to! He loves you like that!

Today is 'Turn it over to Jesus day!' Whatever it may be, take the first step and turn it over to Him, knowing that He wants to nurture your heart through this season you are in. Whether you're in a good season or a darker one, the tender nurture of Jesus is ready to guide you on how to navigate your immediate future. He is the eternal nurturing God.

....

Today's Truth: There was never a moment in all eternity when the heart of Jesus is not for us.

Psalm 91:4:

He will cover you with His feathers, and under His wings you will find refuge; His faithfulness will be your shield and rampart.

Prayer: Father, I place myself under Your care. Let me not stray from the knowledge that Your eye is upon my life and journey.

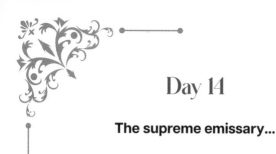

Day 14

The supreme emissary...

'He shall be called Prince of Peace'.

During Christmas, it's easy to think of this season solely as a time to look back at how the Son of God entered the world. While we do remember, we should also anticipate the day when God establishes His full reign and rule on earth. The title "Prince of Peace" looks forward to the moment when Jesus sets all things right.

You might wonder why Jesus isn't called the "King of Peace." Isn't a King greater than a Prince? In biblical times, a Prince was the most important person who could be sent, often representing the King personally. What the scripture teaches us is that Jesus, being the "sent one," carried the full authority of the King to deliver all that was required. Jesus came to represent all that God and the Father wanted for us. In essence, we should see the term *"Prince of Peace"* as the Supreme, or even the best Emissary that could be sent. Jesus is the Divine ambassador to the world. Instead of being a secondary title, this is the title that signifies He has the full authority to execute the Divine will on earth.

In addition to the promise of finally bringing peace to the earth, Jesus promises us a state of shalom. For the Hebrews, shalom-peace means wholeness or a state of well-being. It implies harmony within and without. It is a peace with oneself where we are not falsely striving or overreaching for significance but are at peace with who we are and content to steadily progress toward our goals.

Today is a good day for you to realise that God has your life on track; don't worry.

One often-overlooked truth about shalom-type peace is that the root of the word comes from an ancient meaning to be in a covenanted peace. To put it plainly, your life is in an agreement to stay in a state of peace. This means that peace for us is not dependent on our mood or circumstances but on the agreement that God has made in Christ with us. He is our Peace, and He maintains it. The other shade of meaning is that we have to stay within the boundaries of this covenant agreement to reap the benefits of it.

In this Advent season, there are almost casual comments about the need for peace or the desire for world peace. God is offering us access to inner peace based on Him and what He has done for you. Perhaps today is the day for you to lay all your troubles at His feet and hear His wisdom on how to restore His presence in these situations.

....

Today's Truth: Peace is there for you to receive, so be open to the invitation and stop striving.

John 14:27:

Peace I leave with you; my peace I give you. I do not give to you as the world gives. Do not let your hearts be troubled and do not be afraid.

Prayer: Deep within my spirit and at the centre of my very being, let me hear Your command 'Peace, be still'.

Third Sunday of Advent

Read the Christmas story and reflect...

Matthew 2:1-15

After Jesus was born in Bethlehem in Judea, during the time of King Herod, Magi from the east came to Jerusalem and asked, "Where is the one who has been born king of the Jews? We saw his star when it rose and have come to worship him." When King Herod heard this he was disturbed, and all Jerusalem with him. When he had called together all the people's chief priests and teachers of the law, he asked them where the Messiah was to be born. "In Bethlehem in Judea," they replied, "for this is what the prophet has written:

'But you, Bethlehem, in the land of Judah, are by no means least among the rulers of Judah; for out of you will come a ruler who will shepherd my people Israel.'

Then Herod called the Magi secretly and found out from them the exact time the star had appeared. He sent them to Bethlehem and said, "Go and search carefully for the child. As soon as you find him, report to me, so that I too may go and worship him." After they had heard the king, they went on their way, and the star they had seen when it rose went ahead of them until it stopped over the place where the child was. When they saw the star, they were overjoyed. On coming to the house, they saw the child with his mother Mary, and they bowed down and worshiped him. Then they opened their treasures and presented him with gifts of gold, frankincense and myrrh. And having been warned in a dream not to go back to Herod, they returned to their country by another route.

When they had gone, an angel of the Lord appeared to Joseph in a dream. "Get up," he said, "take the child and his mother and escape to Egypt. Stay there until I tell you, for Herod is going to search for the child to kill him."

So he got up, took the child and his mother during the night and left for Egypt, where he stayed until the death of Herod. And so was fulfilled what the Lord had said through the prophet: "Out of Egypt I called my son."

....

Reflect: We see miraculous interventions through dreams to protect the Child. How willing are we to be interrupted by God in order to change our plans?

As you attend a worship service today – What was the message from the service and the main lesson you could learn from it?

Prayer: May I dream Your dreams and act accordingly...

Day 16

There is a Kingdom emerging.

'Of the greatness (increase) of his government and peace there will be no end.'

As we begin to set our minds firmly upon the wonder of Christmas and the fact that God would enter our world in such vulnerability, Isaiah provides a clear direction regarding the impact of Jesus's birth. Jesus sets in motion something that will be unstoppable – the increase of the Kingdom of God. There are actually two ideas at play here. The word 'increase' in traditional translations can also be translated 'greatness' because it actually means 'greatly increasing'. It implies that the end result will be ever-increasing in greatness. It is a dual idea of something that is growing and, as it grows, it is great in quality. It is also an assurance that the final result will not be weak or contested, but that God's Kingdom will be strong, robust, full, and enriching – it will possess all the characteristics of ever-increasing greatness.

Layered on top of these ideas is the concept that the government of God is not the organisational model of our modern governments, but rather government here means rule or dominion. It's complete, careful, loving control, so that no evil can leak in to spoil or erode it. We do not see this yet, but that day is coming.

One of the joys of Christmas is looking through the lens of the promises that drive us forward in faith to see what God is doing in the longer term. It really will be all right in the end!

When we take a few moments today to reflect on our own lives, it would be wise to ask if the government of God is increasing in our hearts. Our hearts can be like a kingdom, a place that needs governing, a place that requires conquering by the love of God. While we often speak in terms of our relationship with God, it's also true that there's an element of submission on our part and dominion or rule on His part in this relationship. In fact, as in the words of the famous hymn 'Blessed Assurance', by Fanny J. Crosby, we have to embrace the truth of 'perfect submission... all is at rest'. Until we reach this sense of submission to His ever-increasing government in our lives, we may struggle to find the rest and peace promised in the scriptures.

Close your eyes, take a deep breath, and think carefully: Is there anything you need to bring under submission to His loving government? Let it go.

....

Today's Truth: Submission to his love is the hinge on the door to your heart.

Colossians 3:15:

Let the peace of Christ rule in your hearts...

Prayer: I surrender all, I surrender all.
All to Thee my blessed Saviour, I surrender all.

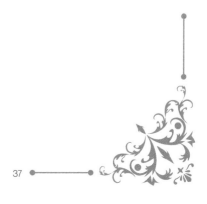

Day 17

God is faithful within our frailty.

'He will reign on David's throne...'

Imagine this scene: Your lifelong ambition for God is denied. The one thing you know will have generational consequences and is crucial to keeping the nation intact is entrusted to someone else. It was within your grasp, and you had the ability to do it, but then God says, 'No, it's not for you.' This was King David's experience when he wanted to build a Temple for God. Just as the devastating message from Nathan had barely reached his ears, David received something even more incredible. David's throne and family line were to be protected and established forever. David nearly missed this promise due to his disappointment at not being the one chosen to build the Temple. But there it was, something much more significant and long-term than constructing a building; he was given a legacy. In 2 Samuel 7:16, it says, *'Your house and your kingdom will endure forever before me; your throne will be established forever.'*

David might have initially seen this language as mere hype or good intentions, but this promise transcended mere encouragement. It became a reality in a miraculous way, thanks to the eternal nature of Jesus. David could not have foreseen how vast and grand this promise was compared to building a Temple that would eventually be destroyed. Isn't that typical of God?

Our plans and desires may seem incredibly important to us until we grasp the magnitude of God's intentions for us.

Check your ambition; it might be too small for what God has in store for you!

At the beginning of the Gospels of Matthew (1:1-16) and Luke (3:23-38), the family lineage or genealogy of Jesus is provided. A close examination of the people listed reveals a mixture of characters and spiritual standings. Some were strong, while others had a dubious pedigree. But even within the family lineage of David, and ultimately Jesus, God protects what He has planned. It is truly amazing how this family is used in such a history-changing way.

The lesson for us is clear: God's promises to you will stand, and His faithfulness will prevail despite any frailties you may have. God is orchestrating your life and forward journey. Christmas is all about how God takes control of human fate and turns it for good. Be encouraged because God wants to transform your story into a legacy for generations to come. It's time to believe on an individual level what we know God has done on a broader historical scale.

....

Today's Truth: When God says no, there is a bigger yes coming.

Romans 8:28:

And we know that in all things God works for the good of those who love him, who have been called according to his purpose.

Prayer: Lord help me to accept a closed door knowing that you have an open one waiting.

Day 18

He came for Kingdom...

"He will reign on David's throne and over his kingdom".

The story of Christmas begins within narrow circles, but its ripples extend to shepherds and angels, Magi and Kings. It transcends the boundaries of the tiny nation of Israel, reaching Asia, Africa, and Rome. The story of Jesus encompasses the whole world. Yet, it's more than just its geographical spread. The gospel of Jesus is for us as individuals, and we can be confident that even if we were the only person in need of Him, Jesus would have still come. But as precious as this is, the gospel is much more than our individual salvation.

Jesus was ultimately establishing a Kingdom, and this Kingdom is much more than we can imagine. Some have referred to it as the 'upside-down Kingdom' because its values and way of life differ significantly from our current culture. In the model prayer that Jesus taught us, we are instructed to pray for a visible manifestation of the kingdom of God on earth. When Jesus was promised to us, the intention was salvation, but it's also about a Kingdom.

In Christ's Kingdom, there is a King, and it's a way of life where His rule and reign are always honoured. The values of serving and sacrificing are crucial. In Christ's Kingdom, ethnicity is honoured and important, but it takes a secondary role to one's connection with Christ. Everyone is valued, regardless of where they come from. In this

Kingdom, the weak are protected and given honour, and strength and talent are not showcased as trophies but used as tools to enrich others. Because the Kingdom is not yet fully realised, we are engaged in a constant spiritual battle. The Kingdom of God is in conflict with the Kingdom of darkness and the spiritual forces of this age. Money is not the ultimate goal for individuals in the Kingdom of Christ. The mindset of the Kingdom is different.

During this Christmas season, it's perfectly acceptable to participate in the cultural traditions we're accustomed to. However, it's also a suitable time to detox our mindset and evaluate whether we've placed too much importance on certain things. Have we forgotten the significant struggle we're engaged in and the deeper values we should live by? Have trivial matters taken over our lives? Have the opinions of our friends and colleagues become overly influential in our thinking? There are more significant things at play than what's immediately before us.

....

Today's truth: Looking deeper into Kingdom values will show us a vision of Christ.

Philippians 2:5-7:

In your relationships with one another, have the same mindset as Christ Jesus: Who, being in very nature God, did not consider equality with God something to be used to his own advantage; rather, he made himself nothing by taking the very nature of a servant...

Prayer: Lord, detox my mind to see clearly what You want me to focus upon.

Day 19

Foundations not fads.

'He will reign over his kingdom, establishing and upholding it.'

Christ came not only to birth a kingdom through His death and resurrection but to establish it through His continuing presence of the Holy Spirit. This presence has been securely established on earth by calling out a people who belong to Him. The Kingdom wasn't a given; it needed to be fought for and established through messages and sacrifice to bring it into being and ensure its continuity.

The idea of Christ establishing His kingdom speaks to His determination to create real change and transformation for us to participate in. Christ is resolute in His desire for us to experience all that the kingdom of God offers. He wants His kingdom to prevail because He envisions a different vision for the well-being of humans than what the world offers.

After the Christmas season, there is often a period of reflection on the events of the year, what has endured and what has been lost. During this season of Advent, it's also an opportune time to assess what you have established in your life. Just as Christ established His Kingdom, it's time to see what has taken root within us.

Things are established through repeated patterns of thinking and behaviour. Take a moment to consider what positive aspects you have incorporated into your spiritual makeup this year that were not present before. During

Advent, as your regular routines are interrupted, make a conscious decision to continue these positive habits in the coming year.

Perhaps there are things you regret having established in your life recently. Advent is a time to break free from them, to remember the higher purposes of God in sending Jesus, and to refocus on His calling for you. Take decisive action to break the ties that bind, rather than making incremental steps.

....

Today's truth: God wants to build foundations not fads into your life...

Ephesians 3:16-17:

Pray that out of his glorious riches he may strengthen you with power through his Spirit in your inner being, so that Christ may dwell in your hearts through faith. And I pray that you, being rooted and established in love...

Prayer: Establish the things that bring life to me, and give me the courage to break off the things that don't.

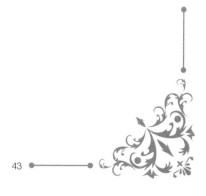

Day 20

Underneath are the everlasting arms.

*'He will reign ... and over his kingdom,
establishing and upholding it.'*

The ministry of Jesus upholding His kingdom is the other side of the coin to Him establishing it. While establishing His kingdom means making room for it to grow and thrive, upholding it is the ongoing work of ensuring it is sustained and healthy. Some might think of this ministry as something done quietly in the background, with God working diligently to ensure that things run as they should. Indeed, God is always at work to protect and strengthen His kingdom and His people.

However, the ministry that the Son has of upholding the Kingdom of His people is also done in active ways, and not just secretly in the background of our lives. Jesus sustains and upholds His followers by feeding them with the right things. Isaiah 50:4 says, *'The Sovereign Lord has given me a well-instructed tongue, to know the word that sustains the weary. He wakens me morning by morning, wakens my ear to listen like one being instructed.'* Rather than just reading the bible, we need to ask ourselves what is the 'now truth' that God is sharing with us. Are there specific passages or Spirit-inspired thoughts that we need to focus on today?

The root of the word 'upholding' also carries the meaning of comfort. We find sustenance when we draw strength and comfort from what Jesus has done for us and His character and intentions for our lives. Like a mother comforting her child, God wants to reassure you of His best intentions for you. Recognising this truth brings sustaining strength.

Jesus upholds His kingdom through His active word to us. His promises are His active words that can impact our lives. God's promises come alive and infuse us with life when we claim them and live in them. We must not think that God's promises only work or come true when there is a result that proves them. We miss the power of God's promises when we only want to see their fulfilment or completion. Here is a very important lesson: God's promises fill you with strength even before they are fulfilled, if you reach out in faith to move towards them and believe them. They are like parcels of spiritual energy to your soul, even when they have not come to completion. The faith we exercise in claiming these promises recycles into strength and becomes the catalyst for God's activity in our lives. Look to the promises you need now and step out in faith toward them.

....

Today's truth: Jesus actively upholds us by His active word and His finished work, so be open to how He wants to give you strength.

Hebrews 1:3:

The Son is the radiance of God's glory and the exact representation of his being, sustaining all things by his powerful word. After he had provided purification for sins, he sat down at the right hand of the Majesty in heaven.

Prayer: I have a need and You have a promise – I now apply that promise to my need.

Day 21

It's all backed up by who He is, not just by what He can do.

'He will reign on David's throne and over his kingdom, establishing and upholding it with justice and righteousness'.

There are some believers who think that God can establish and uphold what He does because He is the strongest person in the room. It is true that God is all powerful and as such, can use His power to make sure things happen. But this is not the core reason or method from which God operates in strengthening us. First and foremost He operates from His just and righteous character. From the very core and essence of His being, God wants to do the right thing and be the right person to us. It is from the character of God that He causes everything else to happen. It is this character that He wants to inject into us.

While it's true that we gradually become more Christ-like as we immerse ourselves in the Word of God and surround ourselves with godly influences, there is a deeper truth to grasp as Kingdom people. When we come to Christ, He imputes or fuses our inner nature with His righteousness, so that we could think in a just manner and act in a righteous way. When we come to Christ, He imputes or fuses our inner nature with His righteousness. He injects His righteous character into our spiritual being and dwells within us through His Spirit. This transformation is fundamental to our identity as believers. Romans 5:17 tells us *'how much more will those who receive God's abundant provision grace and the gift of righteousness reign in life through the one man Jesus Christ.'* God has given us grace to live, even reign in this life for Him!

God operates from His character. He has equipped us so that our character can be moulded and changed. It's not merely our effort, but a profound work God initiated in us at salvation, enabling our character to reflect Christ. Our response is to yield to His influence, to be malleable and open to His moulding.

The focus is on character transformation because it's His character from which He operates. God is just, always rendering fair and sound judgments, and He is righteous, consistently doing what is right and thinking what is right. His desire is for us to operate from the character He is forming within us. Before you act, consider: Is this fair? Is this right? This is how the Kingdom within you is established and upheld.

....

Today's truth: Your character is God's prize – His character is your gift.

Micah 6:8:

He has shown you, O mortal, what is good. And what does the Lord require of you? To act justly and to love mercy and to walk humbly with your God.

Prayer: Lord, in the words of Keith Green, I ask you to 'Make my life a prayer to You I want to do what You want me to, no empty words and no white lies, no token prayer no compromise.'

Fourth Sunday of Advent

Read the Christmas story and reflect...

Luke 2:22-38.

*W*hen the time came for the purification rites required by the Law of Moses, Joseph and Mary took him to Jerusalem to present him to the Lord (as it is written in the Law of the Lord, "Every firstborn male is to be consecrated to the Lord"), and to offer a sacrifice in keeping with what is said in the Law of the Lord: "a pair of doves or two young pigeons." Now there was a man in Jerusalem called Simeon, who was righteous and devout. He was waiting for the consolation of Israel, and the Holy Spirit was on him. It had been revealed to him by the Holy Spirit that he would not die before he had seen the Lord's Messiah. Moved by the Spirit, he went into the temple courts. When the parents brought in the child Jesus to do for him what the custom of the Law required, Simeon took him in his arms and praised God, saying:

> "Sovereign Lord, as you have promised,
> you may now dismiss your servant in peace.
> For my eyes have seen your salvation,
> which you have prepared in the sight of all nations:
> a light for revelation to the Gentiles,
> and the glory of your people Israel."

The child's father and mother marvelled at what was said about him. Then Simeon blessed them and said to Mary, his mother: "This child is destined to cause the falling and rising of many in Israel, and to be a sign that will be spoken against, so that the thoughts of many hearts will

be revealed. And a sword will pierce your own soul too."
There was also a prophet, Anna, the daughter of Penuel,
of the tribe of Asher. She was very old; she had lived with
her husband seven years after her marriage, and then
was a widow until she was eighty-four. She never left the
temple but worshiped night and day, fasting and praying.
Coming up to them at that very moment, she gave thanks
to God and spoke about the child to all who were looking
forward to the redemption of Jerusalem.

....

Reflect: God arranged these two special people to speak over the life of Jesus. What are you speaking over your life? Advent is a season to realise the labels we carry are overcome in Jesus.

As you attend a worship service today – What was the message from the service and the main lesson you could learn from it?

Prayer: Let the Light of Christmas speak a new story over my life.

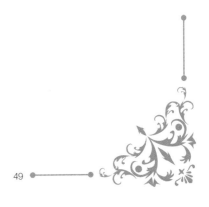

Day 23

He is jealous for me...

'The zeal of the Lord Almighty will accomplish this.'

God is not neutral about you. When we think of the Christmas carol 'Silent night', as beautiful as it is, we could be lulled into a false sense of passive serenity, as we sing 'all is calm all is bright... holy infant so tender and mild... radiant beams from thy holy face...'. This is all very lovely, but God zealously sent Jesus into the world on a mission. Imagine you are so committed to making something happen that you sacrifice the most loved and precious thing you have. This is the zeal that God had; He sent His most beloved and precious gift on a mission, a mission fuelled by His unwavering love for you as an individual.

The are two ideas resident in the zeal of the Lord. Firstly, the word means that God is intensely jealous over you as an individual. He does not want anyone else to have more of your affection than Him. He is a very jealous God; it is an intense characteristic about Him. He makes no excuses for this jealously. He envies your heart; He does not want to share the place that He is supposed to have in your being. Secondly, it's the idea that this jealousy is full of passion and feeling. It is not the quiet jealousy that we often have when we feel we should not be this way. God's jealousy is loud and determined, and full of turbulent emotion. This is probably one reason the original word is translated as 'zeal', because it is jealousy with feeling.

The message of Advent is clear: God's will to save you is immovable. Christmas, with all its serenity and bells that jingle, has the roar of a Lion as its background music. It carries the intention of God that will just not allow our lives to be abandoned. When the Babe of Bethlehem entered our world and breathed our air, it was an unprecedented event in history. God invested Himself in humanity in a way never seen before. He risked everything, and on the Cross, He gave up everything to gain everyone. This sacrifice was driven by the intense love and zeal He feels for you.

At Christmas we have to stop being neutral. Our sophistication and nuanced faith can sometimes not help us. No, we are not to be abrasive or unwise, but we are to be committed and ready to do any adventure our Master may call for. His love for us is a torrent, so our response can be nothing but wholehearted.

When you next gaze upon that Nativity scene, see the zealous, jealous God risking everything on the last throw of the dice for His loved one: you. Spend a few moments renewing your affection for Him.

....

Today's Truth: Apathy is the worst reaction from us as church, to a jealous God who spent His last breath on us.

Exodus 34: 14: *Do not worship any other god, for the Lord, whose name is Jealous, is a jealous God.*

2 Corinthians 11:2: *I am jealous for you with a godly jealousy. I promised you to one husband, to Christ, so that I might present you as a pure virgin to him.*

James 4:5: *Or do you think Scripture says without reason that he jealously longs for the spirit he has caused to dwell in us?*

Prayer: My devotion may never match the intensity of Your Love, but let me be always ready to respond to every inclination of Your will towards me.

Day 24

The Warrior has come for us!

'The zeal of the Lord Almighty will accomplish this.'

As Jesus was arrested, a brawl broke out, and Peter drew a sword, slashing off the ear of the High Priest's servant. Jesus calmed the situation and then said something unusual that hints at His deity. He said, *'Do you not think I could ask the Father, and He would put at my disposal twelve legions of angels?'* (Matthew 26:53). When Jesus said this, He was expressing what Isaiah means by the *'Lord Almighty'* or *'Lord of Hosts'*. It means that He is the Lord and leader of all the angel armies. During this Advent season, we must not mistake the vulnerable baby Jesus as someone who merely hopes to win against the forces of evil. The *'Lord of Hosts'* is the Divine Warrior who fights on our behalf.

However, our Lord does not command the angels to save Him. He comes as a helpless baby and fights in a different way. He fights through service and sacrifice, doing what is necessary to be done. Although His methods are not those of a traditional warrior, His will and determination to defeat everything that stands against us are unyielding.

The name *'Lord of Hosts'* occurs 261 times in the Old Testament and always means that God is the commander of the armies of heaven and the true leader of the armies of Israel. He fights the battles that we must face. Using this name for God assures us that the Warrior has come and will not let anything thwart His plans.

To win, He assesses what needs to be done and does it.

For our salvation, it was not for Him to call down spiritual beings to protect Him. Instead, He chose to submit to suffering because that was the only way to redeem us. He is the Warrior who becomes weak to win the greatest battle of all.

Advent is a time to celebrate what Jesus set aside in order to accomplish the mission of redemption. He temporarily laid aside His glory and the right to call upon the armies of heaven to assist Him. Yet, He did not lay aside the Warrior within Him to do what was necessary to defeat sin on our behalf.

Remember that your obstacle is His opportunity. Whatever your barrier, it is His battle, not yours. The deeper insight into the Warrior nature of God is that He will do whatever it takes to win your battle because He will never be defeated.. If this means He takes you through something to strengthen you, this is what He will do. If it means He blows the opposition away, this is what He will do. If it means He sends you to learn a lesson again, this is what He will do. He is not limited to a single method of fighting. He can use strength or stealth, might or meekness. In the end, He ensures victory. He is the Divine Warrior, and the battle truly belongs to Him. Learn His fighting techniques, such as prayer and character formation, and you will truly be part of the Lord's army!

....

Today's Truth: The God of Angel armies knows the strategy to win in your situation.

2 Chronicles 20:15:

Do not be afraid or discouraged because of this vast army. For the battle is not yours, but God's.

Prayer: I lay my battle down and ask You to lead the way in winning it.

Christmas Day

'The zeal of the Lord Almighty will accomplish this.'

*Rejoice ... for to us a child is born,
to us a Son is ... given.*

From the stable to the Cross, the life of Christ was already decided. God was set on accomplishing through Him the rescue mission and the plan. It was ended before it begun. He was born to die. After the cheering of the Triumphal entry, as the reality of the Cross loomed large Jesus said *'Now my soul is troubled, and what shall I say? 'Father, save me from this hour'? No, it was for this very reason I came to this hour.'* John 12:27.

He was determined to accomplish what He set out to do, He was determined to finish.

From the Cross He victoriously declared *'It is finished!'* – accomplished and complete!

This is a day of celebration and rejoicing. Although we look to the end and the Cross beckons, Christmas fills us with joy because we have a Saviour who was willing to come. We have a Saviour that was willing to be sent.

So, rejoice and be glad that He was born. As the Carol says:

'Yea Lord we greet thee born this Happy
MorningJesus to thee all Glory be given,
Word of the Father, now in Flesh appearing.'

Rejoice *for God so loved the world that he gave his one and only Son, that whoever believes in him shall not perish but have eternal life.*

Rejoice for you are loved. Really loved like no other, with a greater love than you could ever imagine. Love for your whole life, and beyond.

Rejoice for *onto us a child is born, to us a son is given.*

A very Happy Christmas to you!

Prayer: Thank you, Jesus! Thank you because You came and were ...Given

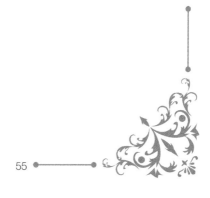

About the Author

Mark Ryan has been in Christian ministry for 40 years, and he has a heart to make discipleship and deeper truths accessible to ordinary Christians. Mark has led churches in various contexts. He currently serves as the project Lead for church growth for the Elim Pentecostal Churches.

Married for over 40 years with a vibrant family life from two married daughters and much-loved sons in law, Mark and his wife Kathy enjoy five grandchildren, who add to Christmas being a special time.

They are thankful for all the blessings they have been Given... especially for the One who makes it all possible.